Resting Bitch Face

Poems by
Julie Quinn

Resting Bitch Face © 2025 Julie Quinn

Resting Bitch Face is a work of creative expression. Names, characters, and incidents are products of the author's imagination or used fictitiously.

Printed in the United States of America

ISBN: 978-1-968563-75-2

Dedication

To Nicole and Jacey, in gratitude for your love, and your assistance.

Without you, this book would not exist.

Table of Contents

PATRIARCHY

Things You Should Not Wear Anymore

If you're over 10, a smile because
Somebody told you it made you look prettier.

If you're over 20, 4-inch heels because
Somebody said they make your ass look good.

If you're over 30, a push-up bra because
Somebody reminded you that gravity is not your friend.

If you're over 40, hair dye because
Somebody said gray made you look too old.

If you're over 50, botox because
Somebody said your wrinkles gave you resting bitch face.

If you're over 60, anyone's opinion
About how to age gracefully.

Let us drop the burden of
Other people's expectations
for how we should, or should not,
Be in this world.

Let us travel lightly,
Carrying only the weight of our breath,
Using only the glow of our inner vision
To illuminate our path
Through this magical world.

He Knows His Size

He's not a bully
But he knows his size.
It hurts,
Seeing other people's fear.

Monogamy

Monogamy is not natural,
Does not fit people like skin or hair.
They wear it uncomfortably,
Like neckties or shoes.
Some grow used to the collar,
While others struggle free.

And yet we wrap it around ourselves,
Like eiderdown and dreams.

To Sigmund: Why Women Wear Men's Clothes

To advertise politics or preference.
To broadcast they got laid, presumably well.
To absorb their lovers like a second skin.
To revel in the delight of not being male.

It's His Style *(pantoum)*

Believing that beauty is in the line,
Not in the woman's attitude,
The artist - so handsome, so fine! -
Paints her only as a faceless nude.

It's not in the woman's attitude
To lob objections at the man
Painting her only as a faceless nude.
She'll know so many like him in her life's span.

To lob objections at the man
Only adds wrinkles and crow's feet.
She'll know so many like him in her life's span.
Let him think she's just beautiful and sweet.

He omits her face, wrinkles and crow's feet,
The artist - so handsome, so fine! -
Let him think she's just beautiful and sweet.
But her beauty is in her lines.

Men of Genius Are Common As Mud

The streets are clogged,
Shoulder to shoulder,
With men of talent and ambition.
Look at me! Look at me!

I remember summer days -
Sand and sweat and the smell of sunscreen,
A hundred tiny voices, each bawling
For his own mother to come see.

Sure, everyone needs a face
To meet the faces that we meet,
But when does the mask become
The second skin?

When does the mark of the artiste become
His mane, his vest, and his bolo tie?
His eyeliner, pencil mustache, and hat?
What about the work?

Books are moldering, unread, on the shelf as
The cleaning lady sweeps crumpled music and
Cigarette butts off of the floor.

A million men learned to play guitar
In order to get laid.
Or wrote a book.
Or invented a technological wonder.

Is that his daughter or his wife on his arm
At the national awards?
What a cow you are to even ask.
It's his work that matters,
Not his personal life.

Mothers will die.
Lovers will die.
Even daughters will die someday.
So who will remember his face?

But the sun will always shine
Out of somebody's backside.
Different boys will shout at the shore
To different mothers.

Books will be written.
Music still composed.
Light appears at the flick of a switch.
And the field of quantum mechanics
Continues to advance.

The work. The work.
It is everything.

Ashes to ashes. Dust to dust.
Someone call Mommy to sweep it all up.

Ad Campaign

Loving trees more than men,
But hating the way the media portray them,
(Setting up a hierarchy of desire:
The untouched promise of flowering crabs,
The titillation of plantation oaks dripping moss
Like lingerie)
She realized that advertisers would twist her passion,
Use it to sell her anything –
Even sex.

We Never Say Most Men Don't

When we say not all men batter, rape or kill,
We don't really mean that most men do,
Only that any man could...

We don't want to think about why
Some men carry through,
And some men don't.

We'd rather hand out merit badges
For being good guys
For helping with the kids, or the house,
The cooking, or the yard,
for being sober, or kind,
Or interested,
For noticing a haircut,
For asking about our day.

We'd rather not consider what
We secretly fear is true:
That good guys might be bad guys too.

In Favor of Good Dreams

Do not leave on your light at night.
It provides the excuse
To enter your room,
To *"check you are alright."*

Do not wake,
Arms pinned above your head,
Knees spread,
Afraid.

A New Old Testament

Thou shalt not call your woman babe,
Or baby,
Or kid, or kiddo,
or swee'pea
Or Daddy's little anything.

Nor shall you do so to your man,
Nor to anyone who is your mate.

Thou shalt not call anyone you fuck
By any name that is synonymous with baby or child.

Thou shalt not fuck anyone who is actually
A baby or a child.

Thou shalt not sing songs of love or desire
To anyone not clearly identified as an adult.

Thou shalt not listen to, or buy songs about
Making love, desiring, or fucking
Babies
Children,
Or adults being referred to as babies or children.

Thou shalt not have sex with anyone who is drunk,
drugged,
unconscious,
or too young to legally give consent.

Thou shalt pull out you tongue by its roots
Before you utter the words
"Come to Daddy"
Or "Come to Mamma"
when what you mean is
"Come fuck my brains out."

Thou shalt take a knife to your scrotum
Before you plant your seed in a woman
Who does not want your child.

Thou shalt roast your dick on a spit
And feed it to the pigs
Before you plant your seed in any child.

For "Boys will be boys" is an
Abomination unto the Goddess.
And he who eschews restraint,
And practices not self-control
Or respect
Shall writhe in infernal damnation
And be fucked by demons
For ever and ever.
Amen.

Resting Bitch Face

Before we were born,
We were expected to arrive
Naturally empathetic, and unselfish,
Putting everyone else's' needs before our own.

When we were born,
The most private parts of our bodies
Were already claimed by men
We hadn't even met yet.

As we grew,
Our appearance was judged.
Was it pretty, friendly, modest, slim, sexy?
Or too big, too bold, too strong, too butch?

Everyone we knew
Had a script for how we should talk,
Walk, act, think, and feel —
And a consequence if we didn't live up.

Now you ask why I won't
Smile as you command.

Because *my* face won't be ruled by any man.

POLITICS

Crimes of Conscience

(For Jim Moore & those who chose jail instead of war)

There are things you learned
When you were young.

You learned that choices you don't want
Roll like tanks into your life.

You learned what price you would pay
To come home with no blood on your hands,

And how it feels to hear whispers
Behind your back at church.

You learned prison is a bit like school —
Good guys, bad guys, favorites,

And guys who couldn't do anything right
No matter what they did.

You learned draft dodging is the same
As car theft to the guards,

And that the car thief sharing your cell
Reminds you of your neighbor down the road.

You learned that you are able
To survive being cast out;

That more than prison gates open
When you walk back into the world,

Because the laws you live by now
Were written in your own hand.

You learned that God is generous
Because the thief learned that lesson too.

I Need a Tonic

I need a tonic against all this...
I won't say 'darkness ' because black
Is lighter than this despair,
And I won't say 'heaviness' or 'weight'
Which would be an insult to mere fat;
And evil is too small and cliched a word,
As if this thing could be captured
In 90 minutes and contained within a screen...

I need a tonic against this installation of fear,
This construction of suspicion,
This monument to prideful ignorance,
This tower of ego we have allowed
to block our sun.

Wind may be only empty air
But it can pull your house
Off its very foundation.

No Kings Day

The whole world looks at your parade
And yawns.

The birds poop on your antique tanks
Unafraid.

Penguins mock your bone spurs
By waddling across half a continent,
Uphill and in the snow,
Then back again.

Camera crews show up, but
No one watches the broadcasts.

People are marching, dancing, singing
Everywhere that you are not.

I would write you a poem, but
Ozymandias said it all.

Political Haiku

Trump insults Ukraine.
U.S. lock-steps with Putin.
Death of our ideals.

COLONIALISM

Cotton Mouth

I'll be Chechnya.
I'll be Palestine.
I'll be the I.R.A.
If you make me be a snake,
I'll be a water moccasin.
Not a rattler making its pathetic noise
"Go away. Go away."
Not a copperhead camouflaged
In brown and yellow grass,
Hoping that if she lies still as dirt,
You will disappear.

No. I'll be the one
Who hunts its hunter.

I know my prey.
More frightened than we are, you won't rest
Until all of us are gone, or under your control,
Until we are rows of Tony Lamas boots,
Novelty lampshades
For sale in the tourist arcades.
It would be fine
If we increased your bottom line
On our way out the door.
But I won't go.
Right now you walk my land
As if you owned it.
The earth shudders under your weight.
I feel the tremors and am afraid.
But I am also ready.

Crush me under your army boot?
Not if I find you first.

22

Colonial Legacies

They come
Bearing cradle boards and baskets,
Ancestor figures and tomb guardians,
Jade, jewelry, and drums,
Ivory and bones.
The sacred objects of
Conquered cultures.

Souvenirs brought back
By parents or grandparents.
Tokens of war,
Or gratitude for missionary work.

(The donors were always so grateful.
The grandparents always such noble human beings.)

Thank you for bringing us Jesus, they said.
Thank you for taking our stories and
Turning them into dust.

Please bury our history in your attics.
Please let it rot in your basements.

Don't take it out
Until the Roadshow comes to town.

Don't take it out
Until you need an art historian
To tell your children what it was.

A Cruise Ship Lament (a villanelle)

This harbor's not what I paid to see -
All cargo crates and industrial mess.
Where are the cottages stacked like Easter candy?

Trips like this aren't exactly free.
I didn't come all this way so I could be stressed.
This harbor's not what I paid to see.

I expected palm trees by a turquoise sea,
Not the sight of some laborer's sweaty chest.
Where are the cottages stacked like Easter candy?

They couldn't survive without the tourist industry
So it really behooves them to do their best.
This harbor's not what I paid to see.

Okay, I know that life isn't always pretty
But can't they just keep that to their chest?
Where are the cottages colored like Easter candy?

Life on an island should be happy and carefree,
We're coming here because we've earned our rest.
This harbor's not what I paid to see.
Where are the cottages colored like Easter candy?

On The Riviera Maya

Everything is right and proper
At the all-inclusive eco-resort.
They have signs urging you not to litter
For the rest of your life.
They have one switch to turn off
all the electricity to your room
Every time you leave.
They sell aqua in reusable metal cans
With lanyards so that you will actually
Refill and reuse them.

So nice to be in a place
Not packed with ugly Americans.
You get to practice your *Pimsleur* Spanish.
How charming to find you have
So much in common with the other guests.
You all own your own houses, and cars.
You have all been to college.
You are managers, or business owners, or
Retired with healthy pensions.
Solid middle class.
Your children are all beautiful,
And smart.

The staff, too, is wonderful.
They bicycle to work from
Apartment blocks on the inland side
Of the four-lane highway,
Dodging crazy drivers and traffic,
Through a back gate marked just for them.

They are so kind, so cheerful,
Attentive to your every desire.
It feels good to think
You are creating jobs, and
Helping the local economy.

Then at dinner another guest scolds you
For leaving too large a tip.
"They don't make that much money in a month," he says.

You wonder, can that be true?
How can they afford admission
To the national park, next door?
But you know.
Unless they work there,
They will never see it.
It was meant for the tourists,
Not for them.

No todas están incluidos.
Not all are included.

Soweto Riots

Canned death,
Rocks crushing bone,
White powder clumped in blood.

Tomato soup
Never tasted so foul
On a Sunday morning when
They should have prayed
For the invalids.

Now they are force-fed
Their own stew.
Chicken-noodle hate:
Johannesburg

DOCTRINES & ETHICS

In the Brief, Sweet World of the Saved

We sing hymn #473 — badly.
The priest begs forgiveness on our behalf.
We admit our sins anonymously,
Most of us neglecting to beat our breasts.

The priest begs forgiveness on our behalf.
We stumble up to take communion,
Most of us neglecting to beat our breasts,
Knowing we have not confessed in months.

We stumble up to take communion,
Believing we have nothing to confess,
Knowing we have not confessed in months,
Fearing nothing we do is good enough.

Believing we have nothing to confess,
We return to our pews, walking upright,
Fearing nothing we do is good enough,
Hoping to pull a fast one on Divinity.

We return to our pews, walking upright,
(*No one crawls abject on their knees anymore*)
Hoping to pull a fast one on Divinity.
We might, if we thought we could conjure grace.

No one crawls abject on their knees anymore.
We believe we are good but do not know.
(*We might, if we thought we could conjure grace.*)
But we are not bad enough for God to give up hope.

We believe we are good, but do not know.
We sing hymn #473 —- badly.
But we are not bad enough for God to give up hope.
We admit our sins anonymously.

Meditation/ArsPoetica

If all things rise from sentience,
Consciousness,
What some call God,
Then a rusty, 1987 Ford Taurus,
Blue, with a scratch
On the left front panel,
And a broken mirror
On the passenger side,
Is one of the faces of Divinity.

And why not?

All of time moves forward or back
From this one moment when it sits
In the parking lot of
JOE'S OFF-SALE LIQUOR,
And you sit looking at it
From a lime-green 1995
Geo Tracker.

A man in a khaki jacket
Raids the dumpster at the end of the lot.
A dry cleaner's bag slides across the pavement.
A sparrow bathes itself in dust.

You are reminded
That poetry is a sacred art.
Naming, like drawing,
Conjures the world.

Observation is an act of Love.

Identity Crisis

Who is lying?

The you with the sensitive, poetic voice?
Or the you who hollers through the windshield at
The kid cutting you off on the freeway?

Does it matter you are a good artist and a bad person?
Would you be a better person if you could accept
Imperfection as an artist?
Can you stop shoving your shadow
Out of your work?

What do you mean when you say:
No one knows the real me.
Do you know the real you?
Who is the knowing you?
Who is the you that is known?
Is there a fake you walking around?

Perhaps you are deceived,
Believing you are some other person —
Someone kind, patient, and good —
Trapped in an alien body
Who throws your shoes against your will.

Deception/Ars Poetica

I write poems to lie about my family.
Not out of vengeance as you might suppose,
But out of longing for
The kind of simple, cause-and-effect life
That could be blamed entirely on my mother.

I wish this was the complete and only truth.

Against a Euclidean Universe

Pick your premises to suit your purpose.
You have so many options.
There is no law that says you must
Take a position of judgement
Hovering above the fray, looking
To a distance where
The lines of our arguments never meet,
Or only cross each other once,
Never to join again.

Okay.
There is a rule.
Written by dead men.
For their own reasons.
Which may or may not have anything
To do with you now.
It's a tool.
Like any other.
Not necessarily
The sharpist in the box.

Just remember:

There are some people better off
In the solitude of a hyperbolic world.
I want nothing to do with them.

Give me the optimism of an elliptical universe.
Give me the joy of meeting once
Then meeting yet again.

You can chose to flatten existence
To an infinite plane when it suits you.
But if you want a different reality,
Stand strong in your place on this spherical earth.
Look to the horizon.
What do you see?

If your feet are planted on the ground,
Parallel lines always meet,
And converge to infinity.

The Feast

Carving knife.
Platter.
Grease-stained tablecloth.

Cartilage.
Skin.
Bones spread on every plate.

And the jackals giving thanks.

MISCELLANY

Suburbanite/Ars Poetica

You cannot read enough *New Yorkers*
To compensate for your address.
Urbanites will turn from you at parties.
They will not come to your house,
Which is too far,
And not on a bus line.
They will send you cast-off books
And educational toys
As if you were raising your babies
In a third-world country.

You could deny your identity,
Wear only black,
Buy your clothes at the Salvation Army,
Burn your synthetics,
Don only what you weave yourself.
Keep the loom in the living room.
Hide your Singer beneath the bed.

They will see through you anyway.

Better not to hide.
Better to defy them openly.
Better to write.

S.A.D. (Seasonal Affective Disorder)

And why not a quick death instead of this
drawn-out death rattle winter brings?
Each year worse, the darkness darker,
The bones weeping, weeping
When there is nothing to weep for —
Children doing well in school, bills paid,
House snugged tight, the kettle on, the cockatiel singing,
And all three dogs curled around me offering their support.

And why not sudden night instead of
Incrementally fading, failing light?
Each year worse, black rats gnawing at my guts,
The bones pining, pining for a way to escape —
The seductive gun I don't keep because it seduces,
Some sweet silent gas surrounding me in the humming car,
Or pills, easiest and most ironic, prescribed, as they are,
To make death unnecessary.

And those who love me, those who love *us*, all of us,
Brittle bag-eyed sacks of dust,
Held by will alone against the wind,
Those who fear us, blame us,
Medicate, restrain, and shame us,
Those who brazenly use love
To bind us to their cold, black world,
Should ask themselves what they would bear
Year after year —
Each year worse, the darkness darker,
The bones weeping, weeping for escape —
Should ask themselves what they would bear,
Year after year,
For us.

Stolen Poem

We mean it when we say be careful.
Tickets are wildly metaphorical
And desperately concrete.
Trouble is camouflaged
And of a prehistoric shape.
The inevitable despair of the artist is easy
As an accident in an imaginary land.

Vampires and People

The difference between vampires and people:
People long to be loved,
Vampires to be desired.

As if either could ever be sated or quenched.

Selling Poetry Door to Door

A hard life -
Lugging that heavy case farmhouse to farmhouse,
Knocking it against your knees and shins,
And the farm wives always so kind,
So ready to invite you in
For cup of coffee, a piece of pie,
But in the end always giving the same reply:

"Sorry, we don't need any."
"Sorry, we don't need any."
"Sorry, we don't need any."
"Sorry, I picked up some in town just last week."

www.ingramcontent.com/pod-product-compliance
Lightning Source LLC
Chambersburg PA
CBHW061720120626
46550CB00003B/1307